NORFOLK TI

The Complete Handbook On How To Raising And Caring For Norfolk Terrier Dog

CHAD BRUNO

Table of Contents

Introductory

The Norfolk Terrier is a small breed of terrier that originated in England, notably in the East Anglia region, which includes Norfolk County. These canines are well-known for their unique appearance and lively demeanor.

Norfolk Terriers are distinguished by the following qualities:

1. Norfolk Terriers are small dogs, with an average weight of 11 to 12 pounds (5 to 5.5 kilograms) and a height of 9 to 10 inches (23 to 25 centimeters) at the shoulder.

2. Their hair is wiry, straight, and dense, and it comes in a wide range of colors, from red to wheaten to black and tan to grizzle (a mixture of red and black hairs). Maintaining the texture of their coat calls for routine grooming and hand-stripping.

3. Ears: Norfolk Terriers are characterized by their lovable and alert "drop" or "prick" ears, which can stand up or fold over.

4. These dogs have a bright, alert, and assured demeanor. They have a soft side and value time spent with loved ones. They form trustworthy companions due to their steadfast nature.

5. Norfolk Terriers are intelligent, but they can also be stubborn and independent, so teaching them may be difficult. However, with consistency and positive reinforcement, they can be well-behaved.

6. Activity Level: Moderate to high; they need regular physical activity to maintain mental and physical health. Daily walks and recreation are crucial.

7. To guarantee that Norfolk Terriers get along well with other animals and people, it is essential that they receive adequate socialization from a young age.

8. Norfolk Terriers have historically been used to hunt tiny predators like rats and foxes. They may pursue prey because of their high prey drive.

The Norwich Terrier, to which the Norfolk is closely related, is often mistaken for the Norfolk. The ears are the distinguishing feature between the two. Drop ears are characteristic of Norfolk Terriers, but "prick" ears are more typical of Norwich Terriers.

For those who can give their Norfolk Terriers the time, attention, and exercise they need, they can be fantastic pets.

CHAPTER ONE
The Norfolk Terrier vs. the Norwich Terrier

Although they are both little terrier breeds, the Norfolk Terrier and the Norwich Terrier have some key characteristics, most notably in the way they carry their ears.

1. Aural Transport:

• Ears of Norfolk Terriers "drop" or fold over, earning the breed its name. Their ears look folded and are placed closer to the head.

The Norwich Terrier is characterized by its characteristically "prick" or perked ears. Their perkier, more alert demeanor is due to their ears, which stand proudly.

2. History:

• These two dog breeds share an English ancestry and were initially developed for the purpose of catching and killing small mammals like rats and foxes.

3. Size:

• The size ranges for these two dog types are very close. They average 11-12 pounds (5.5-5.5 kg) in weight and 9-10 inches (23-25 cm) in height.

4. Coat:

• The coats of both breeds are wiry, straight, and dense, and they can be found in a wide range of hues, from red to wheaten to black and tan to grizzle.

5. Temperament:

• Both breeds are active, attentive, and confident. They have a soft side and value time spent with loved ones. They form trustworthy companions due to their steadfast nature.

6. Intelligence:

• Both breeds are smart and have a streak of independence that can make training difficult. However, with consistency and positive reinforcement, they can be well-behaved.

7. Power Degree:

• Both breeds have a moderate to high activity level and require frequent exercise to keep happy and healthy. Daily walks and recreation are crucial.

8. Socialization:

• Norfolk and Norwich Terriers, like other dogs, need early and consistent exposure to other animals and people to ensure they develop positive relationships with both.

In conclusion, the way the ears are carried is the main distinguishing feature between Norfolk and Norwich Terriers. The ears of Norfolk Terriers hang low, while those of Norwich Terriers stand up. Many other characteristics, such as size, coat type, temperament, and the amount of exercise required, are also shared by these breeds.

Both breeds can be wonderful pets for the right owner; however, your personal preference for ear shape and size is something to keep in mind when deciding.

Acquiring a Norfolk Terrier and Taking It Home

The decision to bring a Norfolk Terrier puppy into your home is a big one, and preparation is key. Following these guidelines will help your new pet settle in quickly and easily.

1. Make Your House Puppy-Proof:

• Make sure your home is secure for your Norfolk Terrier puppy before bringing him or her in. Put away sharp objects, tape down loose wires, and pick up anything small enough to be swallowed.

2. Amass Resources:

• Get the full complement of equipment, including a collar and leash, dishes for food and water, premium puppy food, a crate, bedding, toys, grooming tools, and cleaning solutions in case of accidents.

3. Pick Your Vet:

• Make an appointment with a trusted vet for your new puppy's first checkup. Talk about the benefits of spaying and neutering, as well as other preventative measures.

4. Provide your puppy with a secure and cozy crate. Put some treats and toys inside to make it more enjoyable. Your Norfolk Terrier will feel safe and secure while you work on housetraining him.

5. Yard Proofing for Dogs:

• Make sure your yard is firmly fenced in if you have one. Because of their size and agility, Norfolk Terriers are often used as escape dogs. Look around the perimeter of the fence for any holes.

6. Domestic Education:

• Be prepared for housetraining. You should take your puppy out after every meal and nap. Reward them and encourage them when they go outside to relieve themselves.

7. Socialization:

• Get your Norfolk Terrier out and about early and often. Build their self-esteem by introducing them to a wide variety of people, animals, and settings.

8. Discipline and Submission:

• Start teaching them to obey and train them from day one. Teaching sit, stay, and recall with positive reinforcement is the most effective method. Although Norfolk Terriers are smart, they can be difficult to train if you lack patience.

9. Exercise:

• They need daily exercise and mental stimulation because Norfolk Terriers have moderate to high energy. Regular walks, playtime, and interactive toys will keep them happy.

10. Grooming:

• Get your puppy used to grooming routines early. Maintaining the correct coat texture requires regular brushing and possibly even professional grooming, with the typical terrier requiring hand-stripping.

11. Feeding:

• Give your puppy high-quality food on a regular schedule. For dietary advice tailored to your pet, talk to your vet.

12. Educating a Dog Who Won't Be Broken By a Puppy:

• Instruct your puppy on the proper and improper chewing items. To keep them from destroying your belongings, stock up on suitable chew toys.

13. Being Reliable and Patient:

• Patience and consistency are essential when rearing a Norfolk Terrier puppy. Expect to face setbacks in training your terrier on occasion.

14. Affection and Love:

• Give your Norfolk Terrier lots of attention and affection. They need to feel loved and included in the family unit to thrive.

Taking in a Norfolk Terrier is a long-term commitment, but the rewards of a well-cared-for and trained dog in later years are worth the effort. Have fun with the process of bringing up your new pet.

CHAPTER TWO
Nutrition and Health for Your Norfolk Terrier

If you want your Norfolk Terrier to live a long and happy life, you need to take care of his or her health and nutrition. Important things to remember about their diet and health are as follows:

1. Nutrition:

• Provide your Norfolk Terrier with a premium commercial dog food that fits your dog's age, size, and activity level. For personalized advice, talk to your pet's vet. Verify that meat is listed as the first ingredient and that there are no unnecessary additives like corn or soy.

2. Scheduled Mealtimes:

• Create a set eating schedule with predetermined serving sizes. Free-feeding can lead to excessive consumption of food.

3. Don't Pile On The Pounds

• Norfolk Terriers are a small breed that can easily become overweight if fed too much food. Maintain a healthy weight by following your vet's recommendations for feeding sizes.

4. True Hydration:

• Always provide your dog with fresh, clean water.

5. Restrictions on Your Diet:

• Be mindful of any dietary restrictions or allergies your Norfolk Terrier may have. Talk to your vet about a possible allergy-friendly diet if you have any concerns.

6. Treats:

• Avoid giving your Norfolk Terrier too many treats, as this could lead to obesity. Choose healthy, small treats or use kibble as rewards during training.

7. Grooming:

• Always make sure you look presentable. Maintaining the right coat texture and avoiding matting can be accomplished with regular brushing. Keep an eye on your Norfolk Terrier's skin for signs of irritation or allergies, as the breed is predisposed to these types of problems.

8. Care for Your Teeth:

• Dental hygiene is a top priority. To avoid dental issues, it's important to keep your dog's teeth clean and give it dental treats on a regular basis.

9. Exercise:

• Norfolk Terriers range from active to very active. They need to exercise on a regular basis to maintain a healthy body and active mind.

10. Preventative Veterinary Care:

• Get your pet checked out by the vet regularly. Your vet will advise you on the best course of action for your Norfolk Terrier's vaccinations, parasite control, and preventative care.

11. Spaying/Neutering:

• Discuss the timing of spaying or neutering with your veterinarian. Your dog's well-being and demeanor may suffer as a result of this.

12. Benefits to Your Social Life and Your Brain:

• Mental stimulation is just as important as physical exercise. Keep your Norfolk Terrier's mind sharp with challenging puzzles, fun games, and plenty of face time with other canine companions.

13. Sensitivities and allergies:

• Norfolk Terriers may have a higher risk of developing food allergies and skin sensitivities. Keep an eye out for symptoms of allergies like itchiness, rashes, or stomach problems. If you need advice on how to treat your pet, talk to your vet.

14. Controlling Your Weight:

• Due to their small stature, Norfolk Terriers can experience health issues if they gain too much weight. Maintain a healthy weight through proper diet and exercise.

If you have a Norfolk Terrier and are concerned about its health or diet, you should always consult a veterinarian. Advice specific to your dog's needs can be obtained from these professionals, leading to a long and healthy life for your pet.

Haircuts and Fur Maintenance

Norfolk Terriers need special attention to their coats so that their distinctive, wiry coats always look their best. Here are some suggestions for maintaining the coat of your Norfolk Terrier:

1. Brushing:

• To avoid mats and keep the coat in good condition, regular brushing is essential. To maintain the coat's neat appearance, use a slicker brush, pin brush, or a combination of the two. It's recommended that you brush your Norfolk Terrier several times a week, if not every day.

2. Hand-Stripping:

• There is a soft undercoat that protects the dog from the harsh, wiry outer coat that all Norfolk Terriers have. Many owners of Norfolk Terriers believe that hand-stripping is the best way to ensure that their dog always has the ideal coat texture. When you get a "hand strip," you either use a stripping knife or pluck out the dead hairs by hand. As this can be a delicate process, it's best to have a professional groomer do it or at least supervise.

3. Bathing:

• Bathe your Norfolk Terrier as needed, which is about once a month or whenever it becomes dirty. If you don't want your dog's skin and fur to dry out, use a good dog shampoo. Make sure to thoroughly rinse the coat to prevent soap residue.

4. Cleaning Your Ears

• To avoid ear infections and buildup of wax, you should check and clean your Norfolk Terrier's ears on a regular basis. Clean the dog's ears with a soft, damp cloth and an ear cleaner made especially for canines.

5. Cut Your Nails:

• Dog owners, remember to keep their pets' nails at a manageable length. Your Norfolk Terrier's gait may be affected by painful overgrown nails.

6. Cleaning Your Teeth:

• If you want to keep your dog's teeth healthy, you should brush them regularly. Oral hygiene aids like dental chews and toys are also useful.

7. Treatment for Eye Diseases

• If tears leave a stain around your eyes, wipe them clean. If there is any discharge, wipe it away with a damp cloth and disinfect the area.

8. Skin Care:

• Norfolk Terriers' skin is prone to irritation, redness, and allergies; keep an eye out for these symptoms on a regular basis. Talk to your vet if you see any skin issues.

9. Expert Barbering:

• Hand-stripping is a popular service that many Norfolk Terrier owners have their dogs groomed for professionally. Maintaining the desired coat texture and style is best handled by a professional groomer with experience working with terrier breeds.

10. Shelter from the Storm:

• Norfolk Terriers may experience discomfort in hot or cold temperatures. Dogs may benefit from wearing sweaters or jackets during the winter months. Keep them out of the hot sun as much as possible.

Remember that grooming a Norfolk Terrier can be a bit time-consuming, especially if you choose to hand-strip the coat. Regular maintenance and grooming are essential to keep your Norfolk Terrier's coat healthy and looking its best. If you're not sure how to properly care for your pet, it's best to talk to a professional groomer for advice.

CHAPTER THREE
Education and Interaction

Raising a well-mannered and content Norfolk Terrier requires consistent training and socialization from an early age. Here is how you should go about socializing and training your Norfolk Terrier:

Training:

1. Training a Norfolk Terrier with positive reinforcement is effective. Use rewards like treats, praise, and playtime to motivate and encourage desired behaviors.

2. You can begin training your Norfolk Terrier by teaching him or her the basics, such as "sit," "stay," "come," and "down."

3. House Training: Begin house training early. You should take your puppy out after every meal and nap. Acknowledge and reward them when they relieve themselves outside. Housebreaking is a process, so please be patient.

4. Expose your young Norfolk Terrier to many different people, animals, and environments. As a result, they are less likely to develop social anxiety as they get older.

5. Walk nicely on a leash by training your Norfolk Terrier. Start with upbeat, short walks and build up to longer ones. Reinforce proper leash behavior with treats and compliments.

6. Train your Norfolk terrier to settle in and sleep while in its crate. Put some treats and toys in the crate to make it more appealing. This helps with housetraining and provides a secure area for your dog.

7. Solving Difficult Problems: Norfolk Terriers are known for their independence and stubbornness. Train with perseverance and regularity. If your dog exhibits problem behaviors, seek guidance from a professional dog trainer.

8. Advanced Training: Once your Norfolk Terrier has mastered basic commands, consider advanced training and agility activities. These can help channel their energy and provide mental stimulation.

Socialization:

1. Early Socialization: Start socialization when your Norfolk Terrier is a puppy. This critical period is from about 3 weeks to 14-16 weeks of age. Introduce your puppy to different people, animals, environments, and experiences.

2. Positive Experiences: Ensure that socialization experiences are positive. Reward your puppy with treats, praise, and play during social encounters. Avoid overwhelming or traumatic experiences.

3. Dog Parks and Playgroups: Gradually introduce your Norfolk Terrier to other dogs in controlled settings, like dog parks or playgroups. Supervise the interactions to ensure safety.

4. Obedience Classes: Enroll your Norfolk Terrier in obedience classes. This provides structured socialization and helps reinforce basic training.

5. Continued Socialization: Socialization should be an ongoing process throughout your dog's life. Continue to expose them to new experiences, people, and animals to maintain their social skills.

6. Handling and Grooming: Get your dog used to being handled, including nail trims and grooming. This will make veterinary visits and grooming appointments less stressful.

Remember that every Norfolk Terrier is unique, and training and socialization need to be tailored to their individual personality and needs. Be patient, consistent, and use positive reinforcement to create a well-mannered and socialized pet. If you encounter specific behavioral challenges, consider consulting a professional dog trainer or behaviorist for guidance.

Common Behavioral Issues

Norfolk Terriers, like many dog breeds, can exhibit various behavioral issues. Understanding these common problems and addressing them early can help you raise a well-behaved and happy Norfolk Terrier. Here are some common behavioral issues in Norfolk Terriers and how to address them:

1. Aggression:

• Norfolk Terriers can sometimes exhibit aggression, especially when they feel threatened or scared. It's essential to address aggressive behavior early and seek professional guidance if necessary.

2. Excessive Barking:

• Norfolk Terriers have a tendency to be vocal. While some barking is normal, excessive barking can be a problem. Training and socialization can help control this behavior. Teaching the "quiet" command can also be useful.

3. Separation Anxiety:

• Norfolk Terriers are known for their strong attachment to their owners. They can develop separation anxiety, leading to destructive behavior when left alone. Gradual desensitization to being alone and providing interactive toys can help alleviate this issue.

4. Digging:

•   Terriers, including Norfolk Terriers, may have a natural inclination to dig. This behavior can be reduced by providing designated digging areas in your yard and plenty of mental and physical stimulation.

5. Territorial Behavior:

• Norfolk Terriers may be territorial and protective, which can lead to issues with other dogs or strangers. Socialization is crucial to help them feel more comfortable in various situations.

6. Resource Guarding:

• Some Norfolk Terriers may exhibit resource guarding behavior, such as growling or snapping when you approach their food or toys. Address this issue through positive reinforcement and teaching the "leave it" and "drop it" commands.

7. Nipping and Mouthing:

• Puppies often explore the world by nipping and mouthing. Provide appropriate chew toys and teach bite inhibition to discourage this behavior.

8. Chasing Small Animals:

• Norfolk Terriers have a strong prey drive and may chase smaller animals. Keep them on a leash or in a secure area when outside to prevent them from running off.

9. Fearfulness:

• Some Norfolk Terriers may be fearful of certain situations or objects. Gradual desensitization and positive reinforcement can help build their confidence.

10. Destructive Behavior:

• Boredom or anxiety can lead to destructive behavior. Ensure your

Norfolk Terrier receives sufficient exercise, mental stimulation, and companionship to prevent boredom-related issues.

11. Inappropriate Elimination:

• House soiling can occur if housetraining isn't consistent. Be patient and maintain a consistent routine. Reward your dog for eliminating outside.

12. Attention-Seeking Behavior:

• Norfolk Terriers can be attention seekers. If they engage in undesirable behaviors for attention, it's essential to ignore them when they misbehave and reward them when they behave well.

If you're struggling with any of these behavioral issues in your Norfolk Terrier, consider consulting a professional dog trainer or behaviorist. They can provide guidance, training techniques, and tailored solutions to address specific problems. Early intervention and consistent training are key to preventing or managing behavioral issues in Norfolk Terriers.

CHAPTER FOUR
Exercise and Activities

Norfolk Terriers are active and energetic dogs that require regular exercise and mental stimulation to stay happy and healthy. Here are some exercise and activity recommendations for your Norfolk Terrier:

1. Daily Walks: Take your Norfolk Terrier for daily walks. They enjoy exploring their environment, and walks provide mental stimulation and physical exercise. Aim for at least 30 minutes to an hour of walking each day.

2. Playtime: Norfolk Terriers love to play. Interactive games like fetch, tug-of-war, and hide-and-seek can be enjoyable for both you and your dog. Provide them with a variety of toys to keep them engaged.

3. Off-Leash Play: Allow your Norfolk Terrier to have off-leash playtime in a securely fenced area. They love to run and chase, and this freedom is great for their physical health.

4. Agility Training: Norfolk Terriers are agile dogs, and agility training can be a fun and mentally stimulating activity. Set up an agility course in your yard or attend agility classes.

5. Obedience Training: Engaging in obedience training not only helps your dog learn commands but also provides mental exercise. Training sessions should be short and positive, using rewards and treats.

6. Socialization: Encourage interaction with other dogs and people. This helps your Norfolk Terrier develop social skills and become more comfortable in various situations.

7. Interactive Toys: Provide your Norfolk Terrier with interactive toys that challenge their mind, such as puzzle feeders or treat-dispensing toys. These toys can keep them mentally engaged.

8. Hiking and Outdoor Adventures: Norfolk Terriers enjoy the outdoors. Consider taking them on hiking trips or camping adventures, but be sure to keep them on a leash in unfamiliar areas for safety.

9. Dog Sports: Some Norfolk Terriers excel in dog sports like flyball, obedience trials, and even earthdog trials, which play to their hunting instincts.

10. Swimming: If your Norfolk Terrier enjoys the water, swimming can be an excellent form of exercise and fun for them. Always supervise them when around water.

11. Doggy Playdates: Arrange playdates with other dogs to provide social interaction and play opportunities.

12. Mental Stimulation: Keep your Norfolk Terrier mentally stimulated by introducing new environments, challenges, and activities. This helps prevent boredom-related behavioral issues.

13. Exercise Routine: Establish a consistent exercise routine that includes daily walks and scheduled playtime. Regular exercise can help prevent obesity and keep your Norfolk Terrier fit.

Keep in mind that Norfolk Terriers have a moderate to high energy level, and a tired dog is a well-behaved dog. Tailor their exercise regimen to their age, health, and individual preferences. Always be mindful of the weather conditions, especially in extreme heat or cold, to ensure your dog's safety and comfort. Regular exercise and activities are not only essential for their physical well-being but also for their mental health and happiness.

Norfolk Terrier in Different Life Stages

The care and needs of a Norfolk Terrier can vary at different life stages, from puppyhood to adulthood and into their senior years. Here's a breakdown of what to consider at each life stage:

1. Puppy Stage (0-1 Year):

• **Socialization:** Socialization is critical during this stage. Expose your Norfolk Terrier puppy to a variety of people, pets, and environments to help them become well-adjusted adults.

• **Training:** Start basic training early. Teach commands like "sit," "stay," and "come." Begin housetraining and crate training. Use positive reinforcement techniques.

• **Diet:** Feed a high-quality puppy food suitable for their age, size, and breed. Follow the feeding guidelines provided on the food packaging.

• **Vaccinations:** Ensure your puppy receives the necessary vaccinations to protect them from common diseases. Consult your veterinarian for a vaccination schedule.

• **Grooming:** Start a regular grooming routine to get your puppy used to brushing and handling.

2. Adolescence (1-2 Years):

• **Obedience Training:** Continue training and reinforce obedience commands. Adolescents may test boundaries, so consistency is key.

• **Exercise:** Adolescents are still quite active, so maintain a regular exercise routine. Consider more advanced training and agility activities.

- Spaying/Neutering: Discuss the timing of spaying or neutering with your veterinarian.

3. Adulthood (2-7 Years):

- **Exercise:** Norfolk Terriers are energetic at this stage, so continue to provide regular exercise and mental stimulation. Adjust exercise to their age and health.

- **Diet:** Transition to adult dog food and follow portion guidelines. Be mindful of weight management to prevent obesity.

- **Health Maintenance:** Continue regular vet check-ups, vaccinations, and preventive care. Monitor their dental health and schedule professional cleanings as needed.

• Grooming: Maintain a consistent grooming routine to keep their coat in good condition. Consider professional hand-stripping if that's the method chosen for coat care.

4. Senior Stage (7+ Years):

• **Diet:** Transition to a senior dog food that meets their specific nutritional needs. Older dogs may require adjustments in portion sizes.

• **Exercise:** Reduce exercise intensity but maintain a daily routine. Gentle walks and less strenuous activities are still essential for their well-being.

• **Health Monitoring:** Senior dogs may require more frequent vet visits and specific age-related health screenings. Discuss any concerns or changes in behavior with your veterinarian.

• **Grooming:** Continue regular grooming but be gentle, especially if they develop any joint or mobility issues.

• **Comfort:** Make accommodations for their comfort, such as providing a soft, orthopedic bed and ensuring they are safe from hazards.

- **Mental Stimulation:** Keep their minds active with puzzles and gentle play.

Every Norfolk Terrier is unique, so adapt your care to their individual needs and preferences. Regular veterinary care, proper nutrition, exercise, and grooming are vital throughout all life stages to ensure a happy and healthy life for your furry companion.

Norfolk Terrier Health Concerns

Norfolk Terriers are generally healthy dogs, but like all breeds, they can be prone to certain health concerns. It's essential for Norfolk

Terrier owners to be aware of these potential issues and work with a veterinarian to monitor and address them as needed. Common health concerns in Norfolk Terriers include:

1. Luxating Patella: This is a condition in which the kneecap (patella) dislocates or moves out of its normal position. It can cause lameness and discomfort and may require surgery.

2. Hip Dysplasia: Hip dysplasia is a genetic condition where the hip joint doesn't develop properly. It can lead to arthritis and mobility issues.

3. Heart Conditions: Some Norfolk Terriers may be prone to heart conditions, such as mitral valve disease. Regular cardiac exams can help detect and manage these issues.

4. Dental Issues: Small breeds like Norfolk Terriers are more prone to dental problems. Regular teeth cleaning and dental care are essential.

5. Allergies: Norfolk Terriers may develop allergies, which can manifest as skin issues, itching, or gastrointestinal problems. Identifying and managing food and environmental allergies is crucial.

6. Skin Problems: These dogs may be prone to skin irritations, allergies, or hot spots. Regular grooming and skin checks are essential.

7. Eye Conditions: Norfolk Terriers may develop eye issues like cataracts, glaucoma, or progressive retinal atrophy (PRA). Regular eye exams are necessary to detect and address these conditions.

8. Ear Infections: Their drop ears can make Norfolk Terriers more susceptible to ear infections. Regular cleaning and ear care are essential.

9. Hypothyroidism: Some Norfolk Terriers can develop an underactive thyroid, which may require medication and regular monitoring.

10. Orthopedic Issues: Some Norfolk Terriers can experience orthopedic problems, such as Legg-Calve-Perthes disease, which affects the hip joint. Early diagnosis and treatment are crucial.

11. Obesity: Norfolk Terriers are a small breed, and obesity can lead to various health issues. Maintaining a healthy weight through proper diet and exercise is essential.

12. Gastrointestinal Issues: These dogs can have sensitive stomachs and may be prone to digestive problems. Selecting the right food and monitoring their diet can help manage this issue.

Regular vet check-ups and open communication with your veterinarian are crucial for early detection and management of potential health concerns. Responsible breeding practices, including health screenings for breeding dogs, can also help reduce the risk of genetic health issues in Norfolk Terriers.

Conclusion

Norfolk Terriers are charming and lively small breed dogs known for their distinctive appearance and spirited personality. They make excellent companions for individuals and families who can provide them with the care, exercise, and attention they require. Understanding their characteristics, from their unique coat to their energetic nature, is key to ensuring their well-being.

• Proper nutrition, grooming, training, and socialization are vital aspects of raising a Norfolk Terrier. From puppyhood to their senior years, it's important to adapt your care to their changing needs and life stages. Regular vet check-ups and open communication with your veterinarian can help manage potential health concerns.

Norfolk Terriers are a delightful addition to any household when they receive the love and attention they deserve. Whether you're considering bringing a Norfolk Terrier into your home or you're already a proud owner, providing them with a loving and supportive environment will result in a happy and loyal companion for years to come.

THE END

Printed in Dunstable, United Kingdom

64878810R00047